KAFFE FASSETT
PATCHWORK

KAFFE FASSETT
PATCHWORK

with Liza Prior Lucy

OVER 25 GLORIOUS QUILT DESIGNS

Special photography by Debbie Patterson

EBURY PRESS
LONDON

First published 1997

1 3 5 7 9 10 8 6 4 2

Editor: Sally Harding
Art Director: Polly Dawes
Photographer: Debbie Patterson
Patchwork flat shot photography and front cover: Dave King
Picture research: Mary Jane Gibson
Patchwork instruction diagrams: Ethan Danielson
Techniques illustrations: Kate Simunek

First published in the United Kingdom in 1997 by
Ebury Press Limited
Random House, 20 Vauxhall Bridge Road, London SW1V 2SA

Random House Australia (Pty) Limited
20 Alfred Street, Milsons Point, Sydney, New South Wales 2061, Australia

Random House New Zealand Limited
18 Poland Road, Glenfield, Auckland 10, New Zealand

Random House South Africa (Pty) Limited
Endulini, 5a Jubilee Road, Parktown 2193, South Africa

Random House UK Limited Reg. No 954009

A CIP catalogue record for this book is available from the British Library.

ISBN 0 09 185171 8

Colour reproduction by Masterlith Limited, UK
Printed and bound in the United States

Contents

Introduction

Sitting down to write puts me in an analytical mood. What is the essence of my helter-skelter life and the many treasured objects that I bring home from my travels? The one thing that most of my collection of pots, fabrics and beadwork possess is a bold or intricate use of pattern, usually in strong colours. As you can see, this feeds into my design work. Over the years pattern has become more and more of an obsession. To me it is one of the magic elements of life that never loses its fascination. I can spend hours painting furniture or covering surfaces with mosaic. How astounding it is to see the plainest square box or cylinder acquire movement and lightness through surface decoration.

On the most basic level, with patchwork one is taking a rectangle or a square and trying to inject movement and colour into its broad plane. You can get a strong sense of this piecing-together of pattern when flying over farmland – those huge or tiny fields of various shades unfolding below are an inspiring sight! I frequently find myself trying to emulate the close tones of that landscape of fields by selecting fabrics with very subtle differences and putting them together. Much of the breathtaking work in museums and old houses has faded to a similar close toning. This closeness can be of saturated hues, as in my Zinnia 2-by-2 Quilt (see page 36), or of very delicate ones, as in the Pastel 2-by-2 Quilt (see page 17).

Making arrangements with fragments of existing pattern is a whole world of joy. It never ceases to tickle me how a fragment of boring fabric or mundane crockery can acquire a magic jauntiness when fit together with other patterned fragments to form

ABOVE This display of nails and screws in a market in Vietnam looks like a carpet of jewels. It reminds us what a versatile motif the simple square is. RIGHT My Striped Venetian Tile Quilt shows the square used as the basis for a design. The geometric structure comes from a thirteenth-century marble tile floor in St Mark's Cathedral in Venice.

glorious patchworks or mosaics – foreign worlds joining to create delicious hybrids. It is not knowing what will happen until we try a certain combination that makes the process so exciting when it works. Not only works, but sparks, making each of the patterns livelier and more handsome in their relating.

Perhaps those of us who love this colliding of patterns are hankering after a lusher age when there was more decoration in our everyday lives. When I visit old Norwegian, Spanish or Mexican churches, I experience a childlike delight in all the flourishing painted and carved surfaces. The rich fullness of it satisfies something deep in my soul.

A strong element in the appeal of patchwork is the abstracting of images that might otherwise get too sentimental. When flower prints on pastel grounds are cut at odd

angles and sewn to fruit prints or crash into other fragments of flowers, they take on a whole new excitement that transcends the over-sweet original. Slotting together organic prints and textured colours in arbitrary geometric layouts produces unexpectedly satisfying results. And this geometry can be as simple as a layout of squares. Looking to the rich past of old quilts, I am dazzled by the never-ending inventiveness of arrangements of squares. It makes me search the world for more variations on square designs, like those found in stunning tile floors or even in the arrangement of Vietnamese nail and screw boxes in the Hanoi market (see facing page).

Why patchwork? Those who know about my knitting books most likely know about the spontaneous way that obsession started. How, as a painter working in London, I stumbled on an irresistible collection of coloured yarns on a trip to a Scottish mill and press-ganged a woman on the train home into teaching me to knit. A few months later I was so hooked that I put away my paintbrushes and proceeded to knit myself a career. *Glorious Knitting* was published in 1986.

Needlepoint entered my life in a similarly unexpected way. Lady Harlech, who was working for Vogue magazine at the time, asked me to design a needlepoint cushion

ABOVE The Leafy Rosy Quilt. See pages 18 and 19 for the two other Rosy colour schemes.

• *Fabric B:* ¹/₄ yd (25cm) or more each of at least 10 different small-scale prints
• *Fabric C:* ¹/₄ yd (25cm) or more each of at least 10 different two-tone 'toile' prints or 'neutral' prints
• *Backing fabric:* 4¹/₂ yd (4.2m)
• *Outer-binding fabric:* ¹/₂ yd (45cm) of one of the small-scale prints (fabric B)
Plus the following materials:
• Extra fluffy polyester or wool batting suitable for tying (if quilting, use cotton batting), at least 3in (7.5cm) larger all around than finished pieced quilt top
• One ball of 100% wool yarn for tying, or a matching cotton quilting thread
• 86 assorted buttons to embellish the tying (optional)

Patch shapes

The entire quilt is made from only three sizes of square patches. The finished patches measure 9in (24cm) square, 4¹/₂ in (12cm) square and 3in (8cm) square.

Cutting

Fabric A: cut 21 large squares 9¹/₂ in x 9¹/₂ in (25.5cm x 25.5cm); cut 28 medium-sized squares 5in x 5in (13.5cm x 13.5cm); cut 152 small squares 3¹/₂ in x 3¹/₂ in (9.5cm x 9.5cm).
Fabric B: cut 131 small squares 3¹/₂ in x 3¹/₂ in (9.5cm x 9.5cm).
Fabric C: cut 28 medium-sized squares 5in x 5in (13.5cm x 13.5cm).
SPECIAL NOTE The cutting sizes include the seam allowance.

Making the blocks

Select four patches the same of the small squares of fabric B and five patches the same of the small squares of fabric A. Using a ¹/₄ in (7.5mm) seam allowance throughout, make a nine-patch block, joining as shown opposite. Make a total of 21 blocks.

Assembling the blocks

Arrange the 21 blocks and the 21 large squares of fabric A into 7 rows. Join the patches in rows, then join the rows.

Making the border

Following the diagram, make the four inner-border strips with the medium-sized squares of fabrics A and C, joining an A square and a C square alternately. Join the strips to the centre panel.

Make the four outer-border strips with the small squares of fabrics A and B, joining an A square and a B square alternately. Join these four strips to the side, bottom and top borders.

Finishing the quilt

Press the assembled quilt top. Layer the quilt top, batting and backing, and baste together (see page 147).

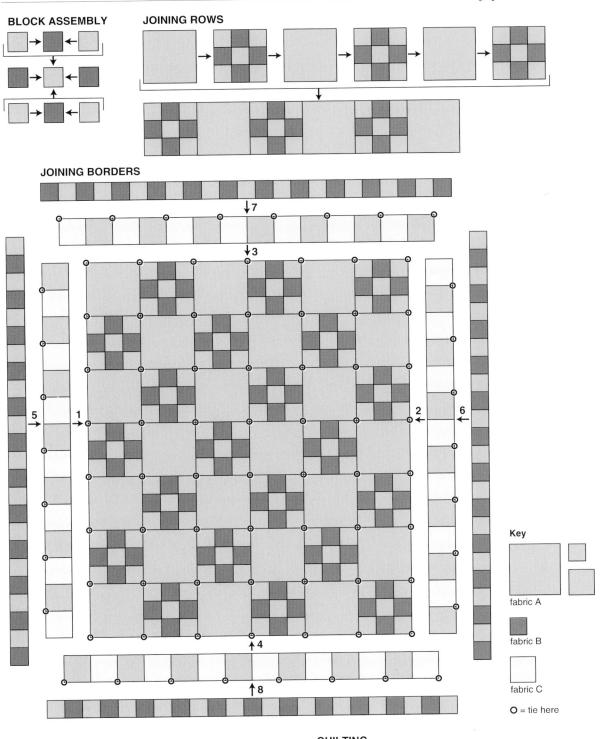

BLOCK ASSEMBLY

JOINING ROWS

JOINING BORDERS

Key

fabric A

fabric B

fabric C

O = tie here

For quilting, stipple quilt as shown in the diagram. For tying, tie through at the spots indicated on the chart, using a 10in (25cm) length of yarn (see page 148 for instructions on tying quilts). If desired, embellish each tie with a button. Trim ends of yarn. Then trim the quilt edge and attach the binding (see page 148).

QUILTING

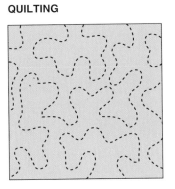

ABOVE The Stamps and Money Quilt was inspired by old stamps and money.

JOINING BLOCKS

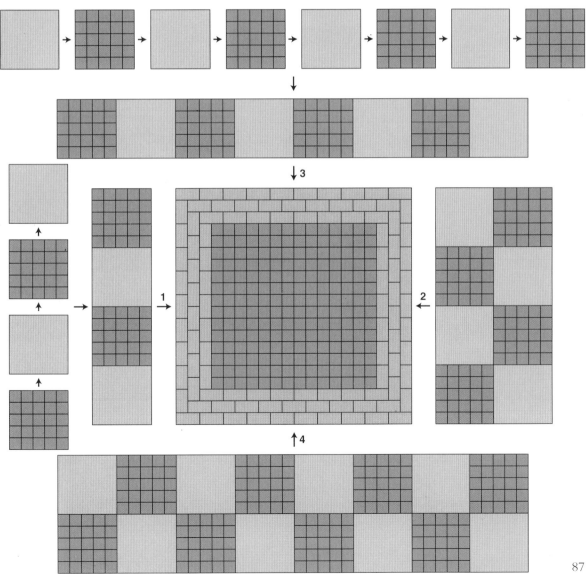

JOINING OUTER BORDERS

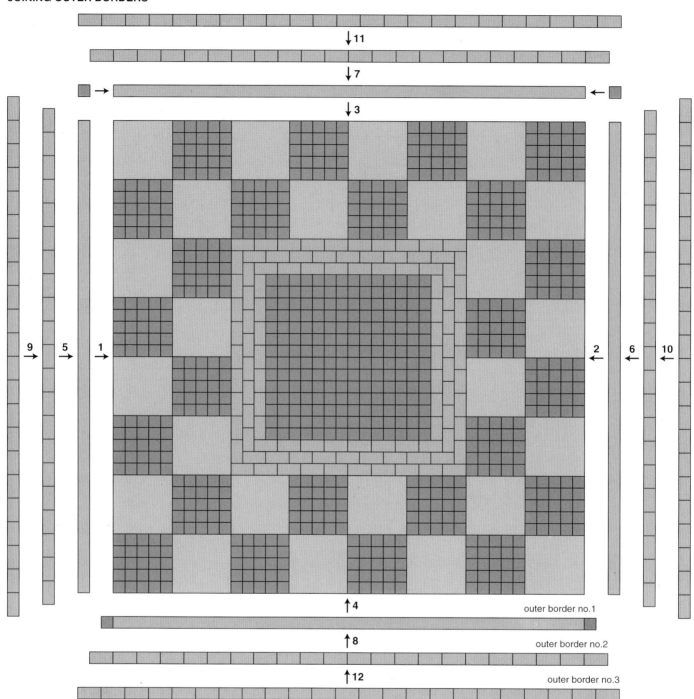

↓ 11

↓ 7

→ ← ↓ 3

9 → 5 → 1 → 2 ← 6 ← 10 ←

↑ 4

outer border no.1

↑ 8

outer border no.2

↑ 12

outer border no.3

LANDSCAPE-BLOCK QUILTING

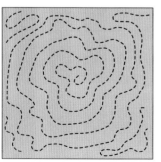

STAMP-PATCH QUILTING

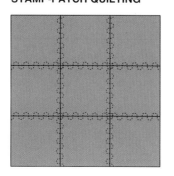

MONEY-BORDER QUILTING

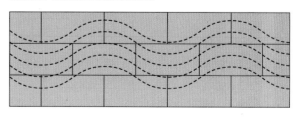

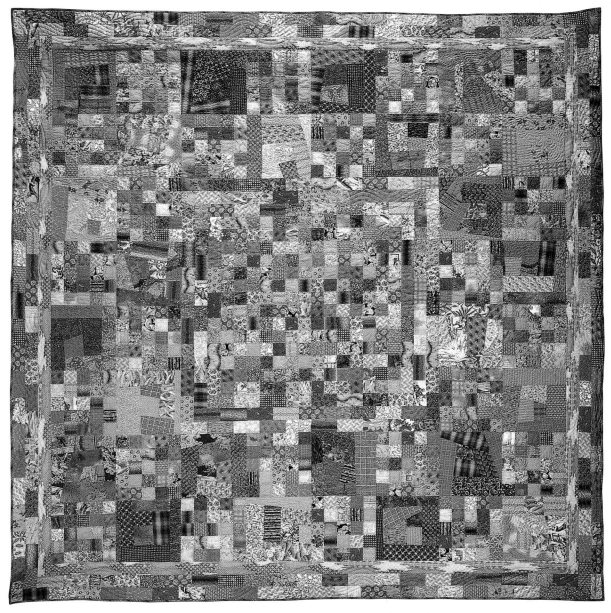

ABOVE When choosing and arranging the prints the trick is to keep all the fabrics
very close in value so that none shouts out above the other.

Assembling the outer borders

Following the diagram, sew two strips of
outer border no. 1 (the solid-fabric border)
to the sides of the quilt. Sew a 'stamp'
patch to each end of the two remaining
strips and then sew these to the top and
bottom of the quilt. Join the remaining
two outer borders in the same way, using
two 21-patch and two 22-patch 'money'
strips for border no. 2, and two 22-patch
and two 23-patch 'money' strips for no. 3.

Finishing the quilt

Press the quilt top. Layer the top, batting
and backing, and baste (see page 147).
Quilt concentric wavy lines $^1/_2$ in (1.5cm)
apart along the 'money'-patch borders, and
wiggly lines that look like stamp perfora-
tions over the seam lines on the 'stamp'
patches. On the 'landscape' blocks, quilt
concentric wavy lines in a circle like the
lines on topographical maps. Trim the edge
and attach the binding (see page 148).

Antique stone

For years I started colour lectures with 'When I first got to England from California, I had to come to terms with grey'. Actually, it was a very positive experience to find that these supposed monotones had such endless variations. Firstly, I noticed that the grey skies and soft defused light made colours glow rather than appear washed out like they can in sharp California light. Then gradually I began to be aware of subtle silver and bronze garden tones and, best of all, discovered the intense beauty of stone. A range of chalky pinks, greens, blues, browns and ochres became visible to me in those so-called grey stones, as seen in the warm camel shades of Bath stone in the west of England and the cool green blues of the Lake District cliffs in the north. The red bricks too were suddenly alive to my colour eye. And the 'yellow' brick buildings, which had at first appeared mostly ochre grey, slowly revealed mysterious shades of smoky blues, lavenders, plums and golds.

FACING PAGE A pebble mirror frame by Candace Bahouth and stones from Budley Salterton (top left) set the mood for this stony chapter. The Marble Venetian Tile Quilt at the Mercer Museum (top right), inspired by the mosaic floor at St Mark's in Venice (bottom left), and the Taupe Lattice Quilt (bottom right) illustrate the effective use of quiet colour schemes in patchwork.

A chapter based on stone colours in a book on colour furnishings isn't as strange as it might sound. One only need visualize the thrilling range of colours in those handsome stone walls in Scotland – pale pinks, greens, grey blues, warm plum tones, deep granite, blacks and peaty browns.

After composing the subtle numbers in this chapter – Floating Blocks, Taupe Lattice and Venetian Tiles – I also explored the deeper tones of Navy Bricks, a dark lapis sort of look, and the bright rose quartz feel of Pink Roman Blocks. The Navy Bricks Quilt (right) has two distinct influences – African strip-weaving, which supplied the idea for the layout for these brick shapes, and Fonthill (see right), which inspired its texture and colour.

Henry Mercer, whose home Fonthill is now preserved as a museum, was as obsessive a collector as I am, and he made brilliant use of treasures in his everyday life. He had a passion for tiles and pottery, and collected and made wonderful tiles with which he studded his house. Fonthill is one of the first precast concrete structures and its Byzantine interior sports columns, domes, arches and a labyrinth of corridors and odd staircases. Every interior surface is encrusted with earthy coloured tiles, paintings or shelves of old leather books.

Mercer was undoubtedly drawn like I am to cultures that revel in tiled walls of ceramic patchwork. Many of his own rather medieval, yet unique, creations are three-dimensional shapes that look for all the world like edible gingerbread. Having realized his vision with laudable thoroughness, Henry Mercer should be an inspiration to anyone attempting to create their own look. I urge you to visit the lovingly preserved Fonthill 'castle' and Mercer Museum in Doylestown, Pennsylvania.

The multi-coloured striped fabrics used in the Navy Bricks were designs I did for the Oxfam International charity. On my first trip to India, in 1993, I heard about Oxfam's work with craftsmen and women all over India and thought how exciting it would be to help create fabrics in the rich colours of old Indian miniatures.

When a year later Oxfam offered me the job of putting my ideas to work, I jumped at the chance and started by knitting a series of stripes of different widths – always with gobs of luscious Indian colours.

When I arrived at the weaving village, I was disappointed to find out that the woven samples hadn't even been started. The colours I had chosen were not available in cotton of the right weight. With only just over a week to spare, I was anxious to get on, so we drove for eight hours to the nearest store with the right yarns. There I completely redesigned my stripes under awful strip lighting in the cotton-dying house.

We then returned to the weavers and spent the next few days stretching out the multi-coloured warp down the main street of the village. Five different stripes were put on the same piece, involving more than 50 colours. The result was a collection that has not only been exciting to work with on my own quilt designs, but has been used creatively by fellow quilters, giving a small village the chance of a livelihood.

RIGHT The Navy Bricks Quilt in the sympathetic interior of Fonthill in Doylestown, Pennsylvania. (See page 21 for quilt instructions.)

Tweed Floating Blocks

For years I have played with the classic tumbling blocks as a knitting pattern, but this floating variation, spotted in an old patchwork book, looked quite fresh. It's amazing how different the subtle browns and beiges on a black ground look compared with the pale blue version of the design on page 16.

As with the Stamps and Money Quilt (see page 83), the cube tones on the Tweed Floating Blocks have been kept quite close, even though dark, light and medium tones are needed to create the illusion of cubes. Only muddy wine tones and dirty blue liven up the beige-brown greyness of the restrained palette.

One of the great joys of having had so large a selection of fabrics to choose from in the American patchwork shops was that we could lay hands on dozens of almost black variants. A backdrop of peat brown on black, midnight navy on black, and so on, made a very rich dark ground for the cubes indeed. I once knitted a version of tumbling blocks in deep maroons, bottle greens and inky navys with black as the shadow side of each box. For a very dramatic dark patchwork you could do the same with close-toned dark brocades.

The Tweed Floating Blocks Quilt was photographed on the coast in the south of England. The tall windowless black houses are designed for drying nets. These long dark shapes on the stony Hastings beach have a medieval presence.

The Jewel Floating Blocks Quilt is a variation of the same geometry, designed

in an alternative colour scheme, with dark punchy jewel tones (see page 120). The third version, the Pale Floating Blocks, has a Scandinavian feel (see page 16).

Size of quilt

The finished Tweed Floating Blocks Quilt measures 74in x 90½in (188cm x 230cm). The Pale Floating Blocks version measures 74in x 72½in (188cm x 184cm) and the Jewel Floating Blocks version measures 74in x 54½in (188cm x 138.5cm). *Note that the quilting will slightly reduce the final measurements.*

Tweed Floating Blocks colour recipe

The fabrics and colours to use are those found in traditional men's clothing and handkerchiefs. The fabrics used for the patchwork 'cubes' are small-scale prints, plaids and stripes that are all mostly monochromatic.

The colours used for the 'cubes' are beiges, steel blues, aquas, mauves, caramel, browns, greys, golds, and sages, all separated into light (fabric A), medium (fabric B) and dark tones (fabric C).

The background fabrics (fabric D) are very dark browns, black and charcoals in monochromatic prints that appear almost solid at a distance.

Alternative colour recipes

Pale Floating Blocks (page 16): The mood for this scheme is a chalky lightness. The fabrics used for the patchwork 'cubes' are small-scale monochromatic prints, and mini-plaids, stripes and checks. The colours

LEFT The subtle tones of the Tweed Floating Blocks Quilt look quite lively against the austere net-drying houses on Hastings Beach.

used for the 'cubes' are peachy pinks, blues, taupes, cool mint greens, sages, fresh whites, off-whites and creams. These colours are all fairly light, but are separated into three tone groups called 'light' (fabric A), 'medium' (fabric B) and 'dark' (fabric C). (The trick with the Pale Floating Blocks colour scheme is to keep it as light as possible.)

The background (fabric D) is a man's shirting stripe in light blue and white.
Jewel Floating Blocks (page 120): The colour scheme for this version is a range of jewel shades. The three-dimensional effect of the patchwork 'cubes' is very subtle. All the fabrics are small-scale prints, florals and mini-plaids. The colours used for the patchwork 'cubes' are reds, olives, magenta, navy, oranges, brilliant greens, periwinkle, browns and mustards, all separated into light (fabric A), medium (fabric B) and dark tones (fabric C).

The background fabrics (fabric D) have very dark purple, turquoise, green and maroon ground with black prints.

'CUBE' TEMPLATE

template S

BACKGROUND TEMPLATES

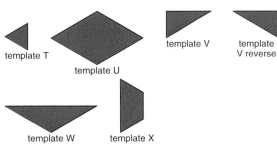

template T

template U

template V

template V reverse

template W

template X

DIAMOND-BLOCK ASSEMBLY

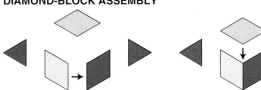
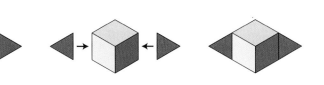

Materials

44–45in (112cm) wide 100% cotton fabrics:
• *Fabric A:* scraps of an assortment of light-toned fabrics
• *Fabric B:* scraps of an assortment of medium-toned fabrics
• *Fabric C:* scraps of an assortment of dark-toned fabrics
• *Fabric D (background fabric):* $1/2$ yd (45cm) or more of at least 6 different prints for Tweed and Jewel versions, or 3yd (3m) of the background striped fabric for Pale version
• *Backing fabric:* $5^{1}/_{4}$ yd (4.8m) for Tweed version, $4^{1}/_{2}$ yd (4m) for Pale version and $3^{1}/_{2}$ yd (3.2m) for Jewel version
• *Outer binding:* $^{3}/_{4}$ yd (70cm) of fabric D
Plus the following materials:
• 100% cotton batting or traditional-thickness mixed cotton and polyester batting, at least 3in (7.5cm) larger all around than finished pieced quilt top
• Cotton quilting thread
• One ball of off-white wool yarn for tying, for Pale version only

Patch shapes

The patchwork 'cubes' are made from a single small diamond shape (template S). The patchwork background between the cubes is made from a single small equilateral triangle (template T), and the border background is made from one large diamond shape (template U), three triangles (templates V, V reverse and W) and a trapezoid shape (template X). The actual-size templates are given on page 154.

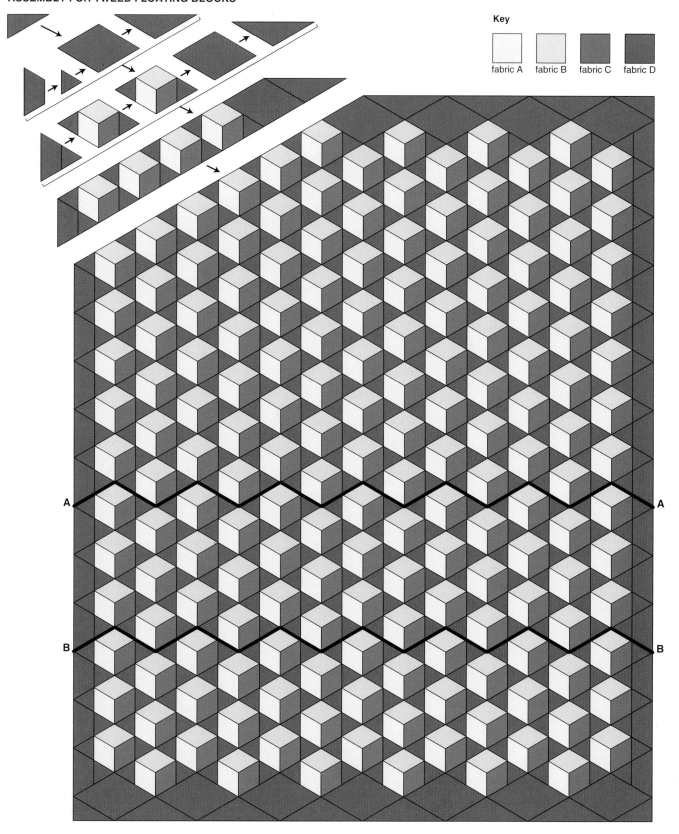

Key

fabric A   fabric B   fabric C   fabric D

Cutting

The three versions of the Floating Blocks Quilt are different sizes. Follow the cutting instructions for your chosen version.

Tweed Floating Blocks version

Template S: cut 175 small diamonds each from fabric A, fabric B and fabric C (making a total of 525 diamonds).

Template T: cut 378 small equilateral triangles from fabric D.

Template U: cut 14 large diamonds from fabric D.

Template V and V reverse: cut 2 each from fabric D.

Template W: cut 12 from fabric D.

Template X: cut 28 from fabric D.

Pale Floating Blocks version

Template S: cut 136 small diamonds each from fabrics A, B and C (a total of 408).

Template T: cut 294 small equilateral triangles from fabric D, cutting so that the stripes run parallel to the base on some and perpendicular to the base on others.

Template U: cut 14 large diamonds from fabric D, cutting so that the stripes run lengthways down the diamond.

Template V and V reverse: cut 2 each from fabric D, cutting so that the stripes run parallel to the base of the triangle.

Template W: cut 12 from fabric D, cutting so that the stripes run parallel to the base of the triangle.

Template X: cut 22 from fabric D, cutting so that the stripes run parallel to the base of the trapezoid.

Jewel Floating Blocks version

Template S: cut 97 small diamonds each from fabrics A, B and C (a total of 291).

Template T: cut 210 small equilateral triangles from fabric D.

Template U: cut 14 large diamonds from fabric D.

Template V and V reverse: cut 2 each from fabric D.

Template W: cut 12 from fabric D.

Template X: cut 16 from fabric D.

Making the diamond blocks

Select one S-template diamond each in fabrics A, B and C. Arrange these three diamonds following the block assembly diagram on page 96. Using the seam allowance marked on the templates throughout, sew the two bottom diamond patches together, then stitch the top diamond patch to the two joined patches using a set-in seam (see page 145). Sew a template-T background triangle to each side of the cube (positioning the stripes for the Pale version at random).

Make a total of 175 diamond blocks for the Tweed version, 136 for the Pale version and 97 for the Jewel version.

SPECIAL NOTE The position of the light side of the 'cube' can be either on the right or left side, but should remain consistent throughout the quilt to give the illusion that the 'light source' is coming from a single direction.

Arranging the patches

Following the diagram on page 97, arrange the centre of the quilt. Select 6 diamond blocks and arrange them in a horizontal row. Then take 7 diamond blocks and arrange them in the next horizontal row between the diamonds of the first row.

Continue in this way, arranging horizontal rows with 6 and 7 diamond blocks alternately, until there are a total of 27 rows for the Tweed version, 21 for the Pale version or 15 for the Jewel version. (The 'cubes' go to the bold line AA for the Jewel version and to the bold line BB for the Pale version).

Arrange 7 template-U diamonds and 6 template-W triangles across the top of the quilt and across the bottom of the quilt. Arrange the template-V and template-V reverse triangles in the four corners, then arrange the template-T and template-X patches along the sides of the quilt.

Assembling the patches

Following the diagram, sew the border patches and blocks together in diagonal rows. Join the diagonal rows together.

Finishing the quilt

Press the quilt top. Layer the quilt top, batting and backing, and baste (see page 147).

For the Tweed version, quilt in-the-ditch in the border seams. Then stipple quilt (see page 71) the background triangles.

QUILTING FOR PALE FLOATING BLOCKS

QUILTING FOR JEWEL FLOATING BLOCKS

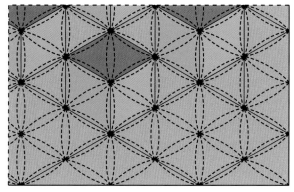

For the Pale version, quilt the background patches with wavy lines as shown above; then tie through the layers at the centre of each 'cube' using a length of yarn.

For the Jewel version, quilt 'petals' in a hexagonal pattern as shown in the diagram, using a dark matching thread for the border and a light contrasting thread for the quilt centre.

For all versions, trim the quilt edge and attach the binding (see page 148).

Pink Roman Blocks Quilt

The source for the patchwork structure of the Pink Roman Blocks Quilt came from a Roman mosaic and the pink cast of it was inspired by pink quartz. I don't know about you, but I feel pink is an invigorating colour. It brings to mind Mexican houses painted inside and out with a strong pink, and decorated with deeper pink, oranges and reds. This quilt would sparkle in a pink room (see page 11).

The original Roman mosaic had a little contrasting square in the centre of each cube. I have used buttons instead as that accent. What fun it was raiding inexpensive end-of-line button collections in yarn stores and flea markets to find those piquant bright touches of colour.

Notice how different the chalky Blue Roman Blocks version looks (see page 37). Basically, I approached both colourways in the same way, taking a pool of blues on the one hand and pinks and reds for this version. Blues and lavenders creep into the hot pinks to cool them down, whereas plums and lavenders give a subtle warmth to the cool blue palette.

Size of quilt

The finished Pink Roman Blocks Quilt measures $60\frac{1}{2}$in x $72\frac{1}{2}$in (153.5cm x 184cm). The Blue Roman Blocks version measures $78\frac{1}{2}$in x $90\frac{1}{2}$in (199cm x 230cm). *Note that the quilting will slightly reduce the final measurements.*

Pink Roman Blocks colour recipe

The fabrics used in this colour scheme are small-scale multi-coloured and monochromatic prints, and mini-plaids, checks and stripes. The colours used for the patchwork 'cubes' are pink, red, lilac, lavender, tomato, plum, periwinkle and lilac, all separated into three tone groups – light to medium (fabric A), medium (fabric B) and dark (fabric C).

The background colours for the 'cubes' in the quilt centre are an assortment of deep teals, ochres and grey-greens (fabric D). The background colours for the border 'cubes' are an assortment of golden ochres (fabric E).

Buttons in aquas, reds, oranges, blues, lilac, pinks, turquoise and olive are used to highlight the centres of the 'cubes'.

Alternative colour recipe

Blue Roman Blocks (page 37): The fabrics used for the patchwork 'cubes' in this colour scheme are small-scale multi-coloured and monochromatic prints, and mini-plaids. The colours for the 'cubes' used a wide range of blues, purples and plums, all separated into three tone groups – light to medium (fabric A), medium (fabric B) and dark (fabric C).

The background for the 'cubes' in the quilt centre is a solid-coloured taupe fabric (fabric D). The background for the border 'cubes' is a solid-coloured black fabric (fabric E).

Buttons in blues, teals, reds, purples and greens are used to highlight the centres of the 'cubes'.

Materials

44–45in (112cm) wide 100% cotton fabrics:
• *Fabric A:* scraps of an assortment of light-toned to medium-toned fabrics

• *Fabric B:* scraps of an assortment of medium-toned fabrics
• *Fabric C:* scraps of an assortment of dark-toned fabrics
• *Fabric D (background):* for the Pink version, scraps of an assortment of fabrics; for the Blue version, $1^3/4$ yd (1.6m) of a solid-coloured taupe fabric
• *Fabric E (background):* for the Pink version, scraps of an assortment of fabrics; for the Blue version $3/4$ yd (70cm) of a black fabric
• *Backing fabric:* $3^3/4$ yd (3.5m) for the Pink version, or $5^1/4$ yd (4.8m) for the Blue version
• *Outer-binding fabric:* $1/2$ yd (45cm) of fabric E
Plus the following materials:
• 100% cotton batting or traditional thickness mixed cotton and polyester batting, at least 3in (7.5cm) larger all around than finished pieced quilt top
• Cotton quilting thread
• 120 buttons in various sizes, shapes and materials for the Pink version, or 195 for the Blue version

Patch shapes

The patchwork 'cubes' are made from three patch shapes – a square (template V) and two mirror-image parallelograms (templates W and W reverse). The patchwork background between the cubes is made from a single small equilateral triangle (template X).

The actual-size templates are given on page 155. (See page 143 for instructions on how to work with templates.)

RIGHT The Pink Roman Blocks Quilt draped over a boat and photographed on Hastings beach on the south coast of Britain.

Brocade and Velvet Throw

The secret of this luxurious textile throw is to get enough variety in your velvets and brocades. I kept the tones quite similar in value while gathering a wide range of plums, earthy browns, ochres and forest greens in furnishing- or upholstery-weight fabric.

I found my fabrics in the glorious ABC Carpet and Home store on Broadway at 19th Street in New York. It is one of the most inspiring stores – six floors of romantic furniture, bedding, carpets, fabrics, crockery, mosaic tables, shell-covered items, etc. There are so many unusual colour and texture ideas around every corner that you can't help being stimulated.

Because of the weight of these furnishing fabrics I wouldn't attempt to use them for intricate patches, like those of tumbling blocks for instance. But for these simple large squares they are perfect.

The romantic setting for the throw is a friend's room, which brings together deliciously unexpected but ideal objects to accompany this throw. What a stunning variety of roses, painted, printed, embroidered, dried and real! Though this room is crowded with visual textures and pattern it creates a very mellow ambiance. The richness of the brocade and velvet throw is right at home here.

Size of throw

The finished patchwork throw measures 60in x 60in (150cm x 150cm). *Note that the metric size of the throw will not exactly match the imperial size.*

Colour recipe

This colour scheme includes deep tones of plums, camel, golds, moss and forest greens, and burgundies. The materials used are furnishing/upholstery-weight fabrics in velvets, damasks, fruit prints, paisley weaves and chenilles.

Materials

- *Patch fabric:* Assorted pieces of furnishing/upholstery fabrics
- *Backing fabric:* $2^3/4$ yd (2.5m) of 44in (122cm) wide fabric
- 7yd (6.5m) of $1/2$ in (12mm) wide dark green grosgrain ribbon

SPECIAL NOTE Do not wash furnishing/upholstery fabrics before use.

Patch shapes

The entire patchwork is made from only two sizes of square patches – large and small. The finished patches measure 12in (30cm) and 6in (15cm) square.

Cutting

Large squares: cut 13 large squares each measuring $12^1/2$ in x $12^1/2$ in (31.5cm x 31.5cm).

Small squares: cut 24 pairs of matching small squares each measuring $4^1/2$ in x $4^1/2$ in (11.5cm x 11.5cm) for a total of 48 squares.

SPECIAL NOTE The cutting sizes include the seam allowance.

Preparing the cut patches

Since furnishing/upholstery fabrics usually fray quite easily, the raw edges should be

RIGHT The multitude of roses – painted, porcelain, beaded, dried and real – make a luscious, romantic setting for the Brocade and Velvet Throw.

design. It is, of course, possible to just pick your cut patches at random and stitch them together as you pull them out of the pile; but you will achieve a much better effect if you plan your colour arrangement before beginning to piece the patches together.

Lay the patches out on the floor or stick them to a large flannel-covered board, then step back and study the effect. If you don't have access to such a large area, you can arrange individual blocks and, after the blocks have been stitched, arrange the completed blocks on the floor until your are satisfied with the layout.

Creating a stunning colour composition is the most important part of the whole process of patchwork. You will notice that both the colour itself and its value will come into play in your arrangement. The value of a colour is its tone – which ranges from very light tones through to dark. Colours also have relative brightnesses, from dusty and dull to radiant and jewel-like. Dull colours appear greyer than others and tend to recede, while bright, intense colours stand out.

Make sure the colour arrangement is just right before starting to stitch the pieces together. Leave it for a few days and them come back to it and try another arrangement, or try replacing colours that do not seem to work together with new shades. Don't be afraid to position 'mistake' patches inside the arrangement to keep it lively and unpredictable. An unpredictable arrangement will always have more energy and life than one the follows a strict light/dark format.

If the quilt has no border or simply an uncomplicated strip border, it will be easy to change the size of the quilt at this point; but remember to cut any strip borders to the new size.

Machine piecing

If you have a sewing machine, you'll be able to achieve quick results by machine piecing your patches together. Follow the instructions for the order in which to piece the individual patchwork blocks and then assemble the blocks together in rows.

The most important piecing tip for beginners is that you should use the same neutral-coloured thread to piece your entire patchwork. Taupe or light grey thread will work for most patchworks, except when the overall colour scheme is either very dark or very light. For a very dark design, use charcoal thread and for a very light, ecru. Be sure to purchase one hundred per cent cotton thread.

Pin the patches together, right sides facing and matching the seam lines and corner points carefully. (You may find that you can stitch small squares together without pinning, so try both ways.) Then machine stitch, using the correct seam allowance and removing each pin before the needle reaches it. Except for inset seams (see below), machine stitched patchwork seams are sewn from raw edge to raw edge. (There is no need to work backstitches at the beginning and end of each patch, since the stitches will be secured by crossing seam lines as the pieces are joined together.)

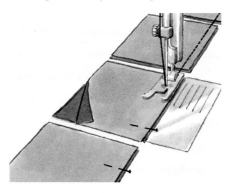

You can save both time and thread by chain piecing. This is done by feeding through the pinned together patches one after another without lifting the presser foot. Let the machine stitch in the air a few times before it reaches the next pair of patches (see above).

Pressing patch seams

After each seam has been stitched, press the seams flat to imbed the stitches. Then, if the patches have been chain-pieced, cut them apart. Next, open out the patches and press the seam allowances to one side.

Continue joining the patches into blocks, then the blocks into rows as directed, pressing all the seam allowances

in one row in the same direction. After all the blocks are joined into rows, join the rows together. Try to press the seam allowances in every other row in the opposite direction so that you don't have to stitch through two layers of seam allowances when joining the rows.

Hand piecing blocks

Hand stitching your patches together is time-consuming, but it does give a beautiful handmade finish to the patchwork. Just lay a hand-stitched and a machine-stitched block side by side and the striking difference in the overall look will be obvious.

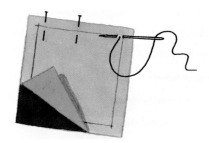

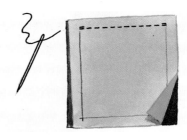

To hand piece two patches, pin them right sides together so that the pencilled seam lines are facing outwards. Using a single strand of thread, secure the end with a couple of backstitches (see above top). Then work short, even running stitches along the seam line, beginning and ending at the seam-line corners (see above). When hand piecing, never stitch across the seam allowances.

Press the seam allowances to one side as for machine-pieced seams, or press all seam allowances open.

Stitching inset seams

You will find that most patches can be joined together with a straight seam line, but with some patchwork layouts a patch will need to be sewn into a corner formed by two other patches. This will require a seam line that turns a corner – called an inset seam.

First, align the patches along one side of the angle and pin, matching up the corner points exactly. Machine stitch along the seam line of this edge up to the corner point and work a few backstitches to secure (see above).

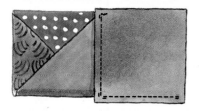

Then pivot the set-in patch, align the adjacent side with the edge of the next patch and pin. Beginning exactly at the corner point, work a few backstitches to secure, then machine stitch along the seam line to the outer edge of the patches (see above).

Trim away excess fabric from the seam allowance at the corner of the inset patch as necessary. Press the new seams, easing the corner into the correct shape (see above).

Paper Foundation Piecing

In paper foundation piecing the patchwork block design is drawn on a piece of paper the exact size of the block. Each patch shape on the paper is numbered to indicate the sequence in which the patches should be stitched. During the stitching process, the patches are joined together under the paper foundation piece with the patch seams piercing the fabric layers and the paper.

This techniques has many advantages. It requires little skill and is very accurate. It is also incredibly quick because there is no need for cutting patches with templates; all the fabric pieces are cut in very rough shapes and trimmed as they are stitched to the paper foundation.

Another advantage of paper foundation piecing is that it allows you to use patches that are not cut on the straight grain of the fabric. The paper provides the stability needed to keep the off-grain seams from stretching. Not having to pay attention to cutting exactly on the grain line speeds up the piecing process considerably. It also enables you to design patchworks with stripes, plaids and prints set at random angles (see instructions for the Super Triangles Baby Quilt on pages 50–55).

Preparing paper foundations

You will need a paper foundation for each of the blocks being made with the technique. Either photocopy the diagram of the foundation piece or draw it on graph paper. If you are drawing the design, be as accurate as possible.

Always use a 'first generation' photocopy or the drawing as the master for the block design and take all of the photocopies of it directly from this master. Try to avoid making photocopies of photocopies, since the design will become distorted. The number of copies required will be given in the quilt instructions.

Cut out each paper foundation along the outer cutting line, which includes the seam allowance. If there are blocks of different sizes in the patchwork, check the master foundation pieces to make sure that they are all the correct size to fit together accurately.

Cutting fabric pieces

Before beginning to stitch the block, cut the fabric pieces for each of the numbered areas on the foundation piece. The size and shape of the fabric pieces need only be approximate. Allow for about a ½in (12mm) seam allowance, and if in doubt, cut the piece bigger rather than smaller.

The numbered side of the foundation paper is the wrong side of the block, so cut the fabric pieces with the wrong side facing up.

Stitching the blocks

Once the fabric pieces are ready, insert a 90/14 machine needle. Then set the sewing machine stitch length to a short stitch – about 18 to 20 stitches per inch (2.5cm). The large needle and short stitch will help to perforate the paper, making it easier to tear away later.

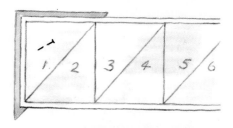

Take the fabric piece for area no. 1 and pin it to the back of the foundation paper under area no. 1 of the block, with the wrong side of the fabric facing the unmarked side of the paper (see above). Hold the paper up to the light to make sure that the fabric piece covers the area and extends at least ¼in (6mm) beyond the stitching lines.

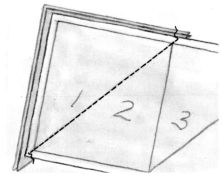

Next, place piece no. 2 on top of no. 1 (see above) with the right sides facing and the raw edges aligned along the seam-line edge. Holding the patches in place, machine stitch along the seam line between no. 1 and no. 2 with the marked side of the paper block facing upwards. Begin and end the stitching in the seam allowance so that it extends slightly beyond each end of the seam line as shown. The ends of the stitching will be secured by future seams.

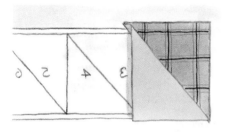

Trim the seam allowance to ¼in (6mm) using a small, sharp pair of scissors. Then open out piece no. 2 (see above), finger press the seam and press with a hot iron but no steam; for small pieces, only finger-pressing the seam will be adequate. Continue adding pieces in this way, joining them in the sequence marked on the block.

After the last patch has been stitched in place on the foundation paper, trim away the excess fabric around the edge of the block with a rotary cutter and ruler, leaving the designated seam allowance around the outer edge of the finished block (see above).

Leave the paper foundation piece on the block until all the blocks have been stitched together, but tear out any paper corners that will make the seams too bulky. Note that the right side of the finished block is the reverse image of

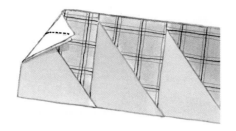

the marked side of the foundation paper (see above). Once all the blocks are joined, tear away all of the paper.

Quilting and Finishing

After you have finished piecing your patchwork, press it carefully. It is now ready to be quilted if quilting is required. However, many items of patchwork, such as cushion covers, throws, curtains and table covers need only be backed.

Quilting patterns

Patchwork quilting is the stitching that joins together the three layers of the quilt sandwich – top, batting/wadding and backing. For patchworks that have a strong design story of their own, try to chose a quilting pattern that does not detract from the patchwork. In some instances you will find that stitch-in-the-ditch quilting is the perfect choice, since the quilting lines are stitched into the patch seam lines making the quilting stitches invisible on the right side of the patchwork.

Outline quilting is another simple quilting pattern that will suit many patchwork designs. It is worked by stitching ¼in (6mm) from the patch seam lines.

You will need to mark more complicated quilting patterns on the right side of the piece patchwork before the quilt layers are joined. The marking can be done with specially designed quilting markers. If you are in doubt about which quilting pattern to chose, test the pattern on a spare pieced block. This will also be a good way to check whether your chosen quilting thread is a suitable colour.

Quilting thread is a specially made cotton thread that is thicker and stronger than ordinary sewing thread. The thread colour should usually blend

invisibly into the overall colour of the patchwork quilt when it is viewed from a distance.

Using a quilting stencil is the easiest way to mark a complicated pattern on to the fabric. These stencils are widely available in shops that sell patchwork and quilting materials.

Preparing the backing and batting

Cut the selvedges off of the backing fabric, then seam the pieces together to form a backing at least 3 inches (7.5cm) bigger all around than the patchwork. It is best to join the pieces so that the seam lines run lengthways.

If the batting/wadding has been rolled, unroll it and let it rest before cutting it to about the same size as the backing. Batting comes in various thicknesses, but a pure cotton or mixed cotton and polyester batting which is fairly thin, will be a good choice for most quilts. Thicker batting is usually only suitable when the quilt layers are being tied together. A hundred per cent cotton batting will give your quilt the attractive, relatively flat appearance of an antique quilt.

Basting the quilt layers

Lay out the backing wrong side up and smooth it out. Place the batting on top of the backing, then lay the pieced patchwork right side up on top of the batting and smooth it out.

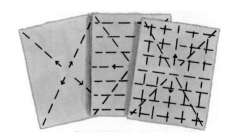

Beginning at the centre, baste two diagonal lines from corner to corner through the layers (see above left). Make stitches about 3 inches (7.5cm) long and try not to lift the layers too much as you stitch. Then, again always beginning at the centre and working outwards, baste horizontal and vertical lines across the layers (see above centre and right). The basting lines should be about 4 inches (10cm) apart.

Hand Quilting

Hand quilting is best done with the quilt layers mounted in a quilting frame or hoop. Thread a short quilting needle (an 8 to 11 between) with an 18in (46cm) length of special cotton quilting thread and knot the end. With the quilt top facing upwards and beginning at the centre of the basted quilt layers, insert the needle through the top about ½in (12mm) from the starting point and into the batting, then bring it out at the starting point. Pull the thread to pop the knot into the batting.

Loading about three or four stitches on to the needle and working with one hand under the quilt to help the needle back up again, make short, even running stitches. Pull the thread through and continue along the quilting line in this way.

It is more important to make even stitches on both sides of the quilt than to make small ones. When the thread is about to run out, make a small backstitch, then pierce this backstitch to anchor it and run the thread end through into the batting.

Machine quilting

For machine quilting, use a walking foot for straight lines and a darning foot for curved lines. Use regular sewing thread and choose a colour that blends with the overall colour of the patchwork for the top thread and one that matches the backing for the bobbin thread. Begin and end the quilting lines with very short stitches to secure, leaving long ends to thread into the batting later. Follow the machine manual for tips on using the walking or darning feet.

Tying quilts

If you don't have the time needed for allover quilting, you can tie together the basted layers of your patchwork quilt. Make sure that you are using a batting with a high loft, because thin cotton battings usually require quite close quilting lines.

Use a sharp needle with a large eye and wool yarn, thick embroidery thread or narrow ribbon for the tying. For simple tying, cut a 7in (18cm) length of yarn and thread the needle.

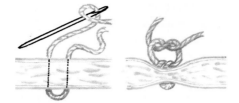

Beginning the tying at the centre of the quilt, make a small stitch through all three layers (see fig 17, above left). Tie the two ends of the yarn into a double knot (see fig 17, above right) and trim. If you are making bows, use a longer length of thread.

Binding quilt edges

Once the quilt has been quilted or tied together, remove the basting threads. Then baste around the quilt just under ¼in (about 5mm) from the edge of the patchwork. Trim the outer edge of the quilt, cutting away the excess batting and backing right up to the edge of the patchwork and, if necessary, straightening the edge of the patchwork in the process.

Cut 2in (5cm) wide binding strips either on the straight grain or on the bias. (Striped fabrics look especially effective when cut on the bias to form diagonal stripes around the edge of the patchwork.) Join these binding strips end-to-end with diagonal seams until the strip is long enough to fit around the edge.

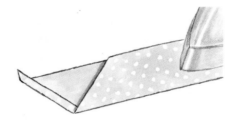

Cut the beginning end of the binding strip at a 45 degree angle, turn ¼in (6mm) to the wrong side along this cut end, and press. Then fold the strip in half lengthways with the wrong sides together and press (see above).

Place the doubled binding on the right side of the quilt, with the longer side facing the quilt and aligning the raw edges. Stitch from the second folded edge on the binding ¼in (6mm) from the edge up to ¼in (6mm) from the first

corner (see above). Make a few backstitches and cut the thread ends.

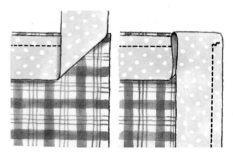

Fold the binding up, making a 45 degree angle (see above left). Keeping the diagonal fold in place, fold the binding back down and align the edge with the next side of the quilt. Beginning at the point where the last stitching ended, stitch down the next side (see above right).

Continue stitching the binding in place all around the edge in this way, tucking the end inside the beginning of the binding (see above).

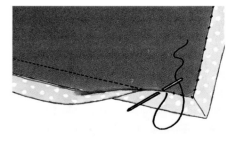

Turn the folded edge of the binding to the back. Hand stitch in place, folding a mitre at each corner (see above).